TRINITY REPERTOIRE LIBRARY

VIOLA

All Sorts

GRADES 2–3

Selected and edited by Mary Cohen

Piano arrangements by David Wright

PIANO ACCOMPANIMENT

TRINITY COLLEGE LONDON
89 Albert Embankment London SE1 7TP

Contents

Published by:
Trinity College London
89 Albert Embankment
London SE1 7TP UK
T +44 (0)20 7820 6100
F +44 (0)20 7820 6161
E music@trinityguildhall.co.uk
www.trinityguildhall.co.uk

Copyright © 2009 Faber Music Ltd. and Trinity College London
TG008480 ISMN 979-0-57038-061-9

Printed in England by Halstan & Co. Ltd, Amersham, Bucks.
All Trinity Guildhall publications are available from your local music shop,
and may also be ordered directly from our exclusive distributor:

Faber Music Distribution Ltd, Burnt Mill, Elizabeth Way, Harlow CM20 2HX
T +44 (0)1279 82 89 82
F +44 (0)1279 82 89 83
sales@fabermusic.com
www.fabermusic.com

PRINCE OF DENMARK'S MARCH

Imagine a grand occasion at court when you play this, with everyone
dressed in fine clothes and music provided by trumpets and drums.

Jeremiah Clarke
(c.1670–1707)

THEME FROM POLOVTSIAN DANCES

The Russian composer Borodin wrote this piece as part of a ballet scene
within his opera *Prince Igor*.

Alexander Borodin
(1833–1887)

ROBIN'S RETREAT

This piece is based on a popular sixteenth-century dance style called an allemande.
Two lines of people dance towards each other, circle around and cross to the other side.

Pam Wedgwood

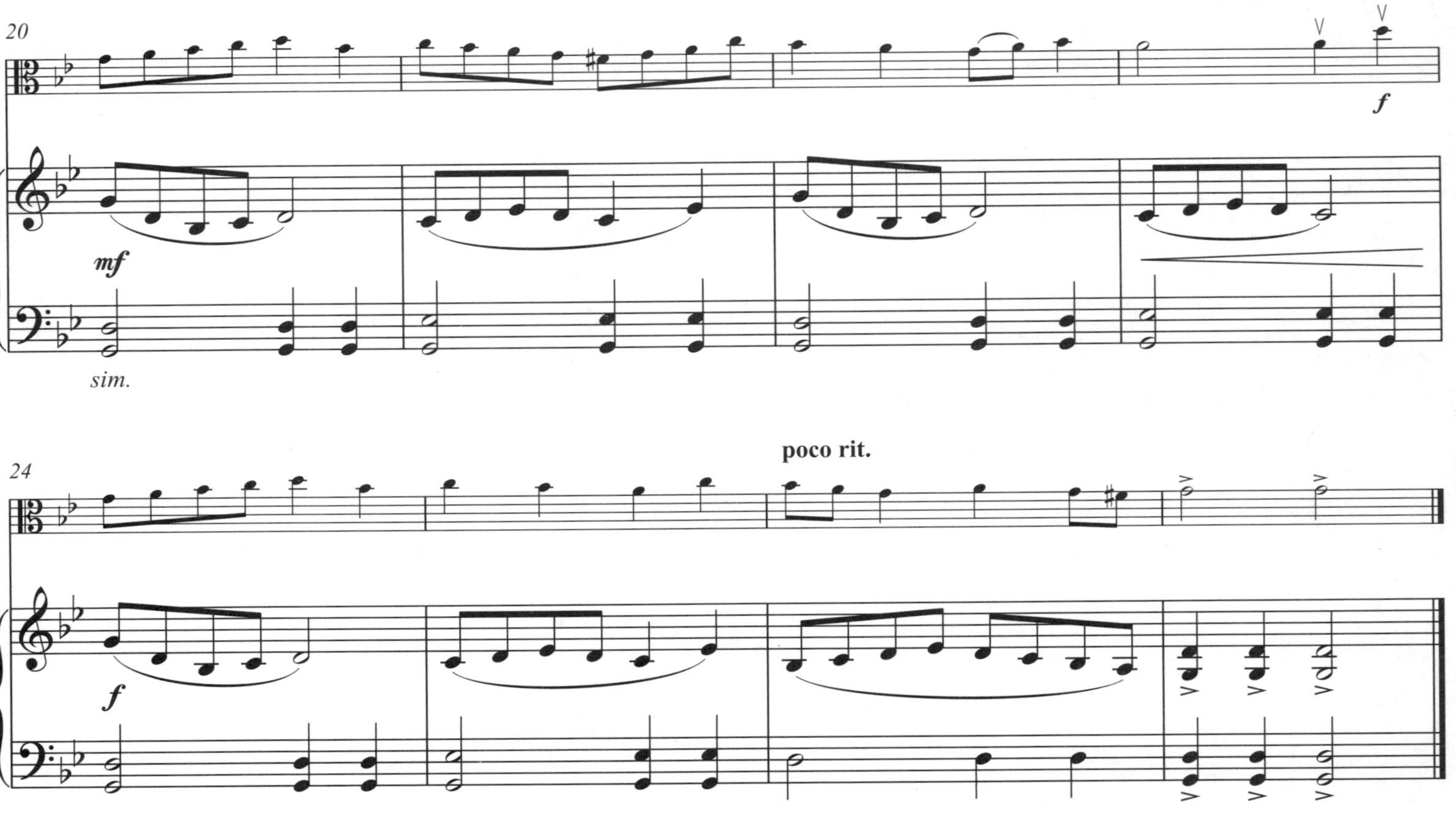
20
mf
sim.
f
24
poco rit.
f

OUT 'N' ABOUT RAG

Mary Cohen

Music in 'ragged' time means that some beats are longer or shorter than you might expect. The most famous ragtime composer was Scott Joplin, who said 'you should never play them quick'.

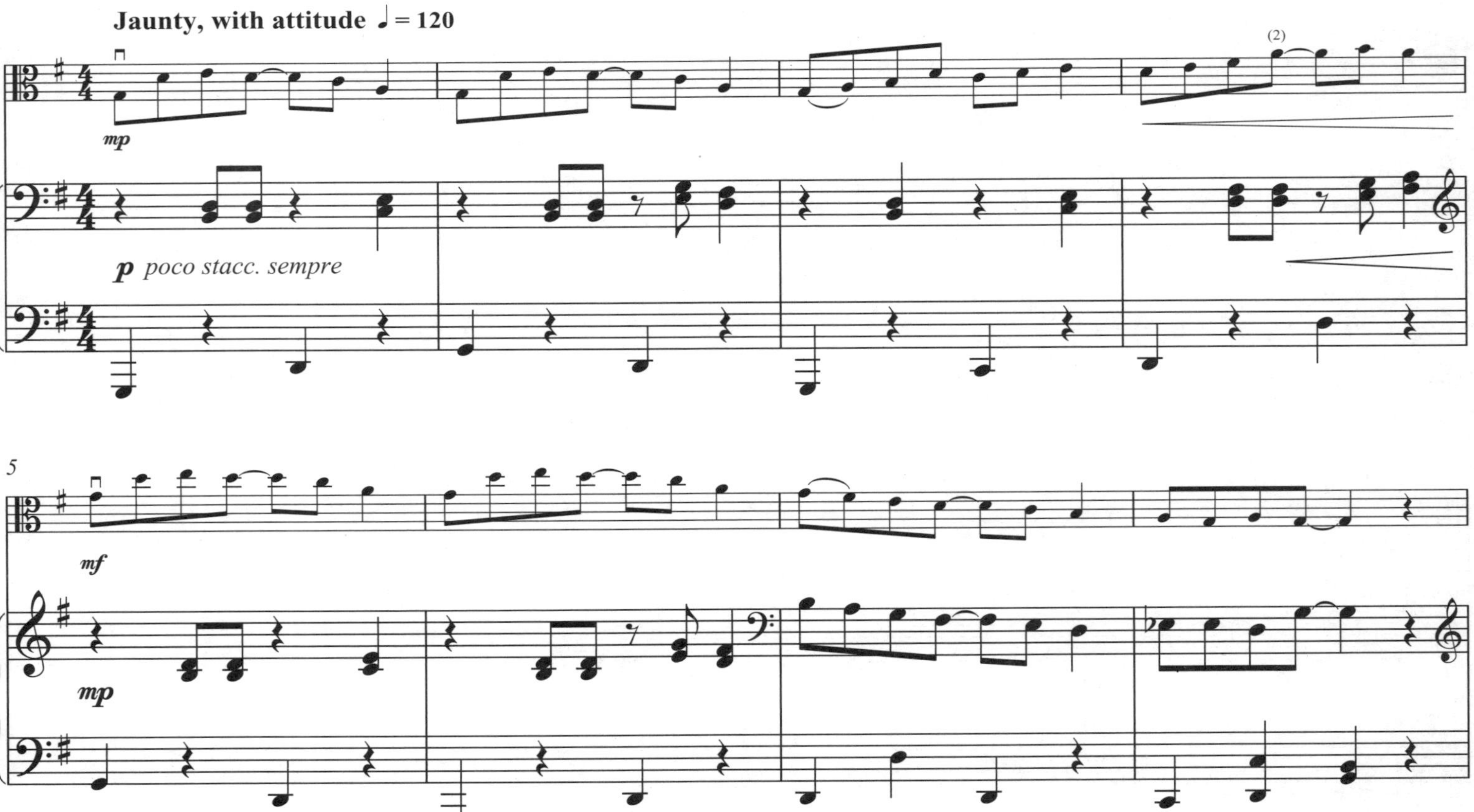
Jaunty, with attitude ♩ = 120
mp
(2)
p poco stacc. sempre
5
mf
mp

LISON DORMAIT

This title means 'Lison was sleeping'. Imagine someone
tiptoeing past in bars 9 to 16, trying not to wake Lison.

Wolfgang Amadeus Mozart
(1756–1791)

MINUET

This was originally written for the baryton – a popular instrument in
Haydn's day. It had one set of strings to be plucked or bowed and
another set under the fingerboard which vibrated in sympathy.

Franz Joseph Haydn
(1732–1809)

DANCE OF THE BLESSED SPIRITS

This is one of Gluck's best-known pieces. It comes from his opera
Orpheus and Euridice.

Christoph von Gluck
(1714–1787)

SARABANDE

Corelli was an Italian violinist and composer. Although he wrote only a few works, his style of violin playing set new standards and influenced many composers.

Arcangelo Corelli
(1653–1713)

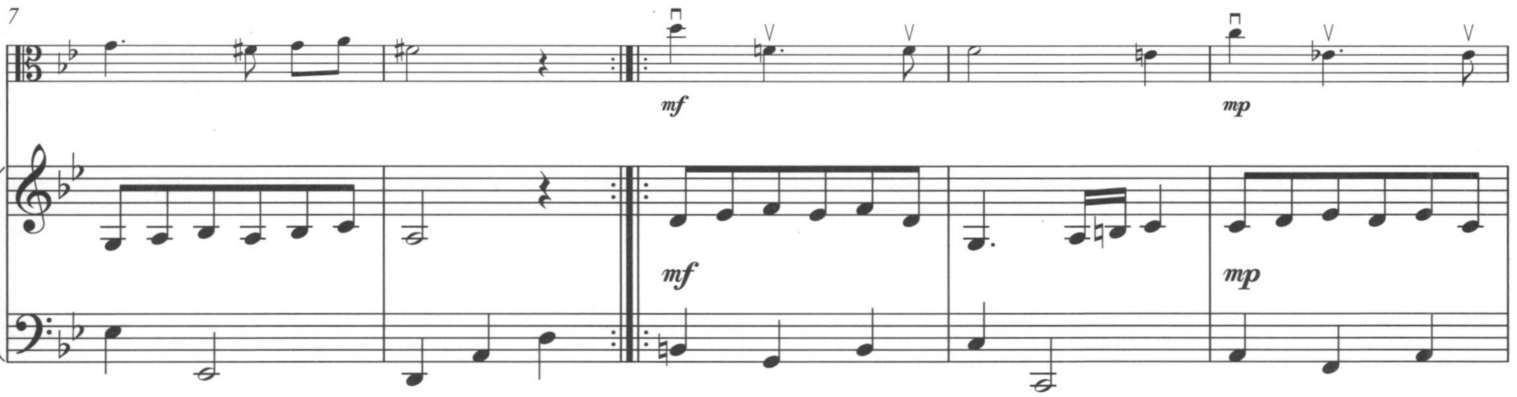

MARCH FROM L'ARLÉSIENNE

This tune is based on a traditional carol from Provence called *The Three Kings.*
Imagine it's being played in a procession by a pipe and drum – fading into the
distance at the end.

Georges Bizet
(1838–1875)

PAVANE

Fauré wrote this piece for a big party in Paris. The guests dressed up in
historical costumes and danced to music played by a hidden band of musicians.

Gabriel Fauré
(1845–1924)

GAVOTTE *FROM SUITE IN D*

Johann Sebastian Bach
(1685–1750)

The Bach family produced several generations of musicians, of whom Johann Sebastian was the most famous. As well as being a great composer, J S Bach was a virtuoso organist.

THE DEATH OF ÅSE *FROM PEER GYNT SUITE*

Grieg was a Norwegian composer and pianist who had a great interest in his native folk music. Perhaps because of this, his music often contains unusual harmonies.

Edvard Grieg
(1843–1907)

THE BIRDS GATHER AT DUSK

When the farmers hear the birds begin to gather at dusk,
it's the signal for the end of the long working day.

Mary Cohen
after a Chinese folk song

RONDO THEME *from op. 48*

Whilst a pupil of Haydn's, Pleyel wrote a piece that so impressed Haydn's
patron, that the elder musician was presented with a carriage 'for having such
a good pupil'. How fair was that?

Ignaz Pleyel
(1757–1831)

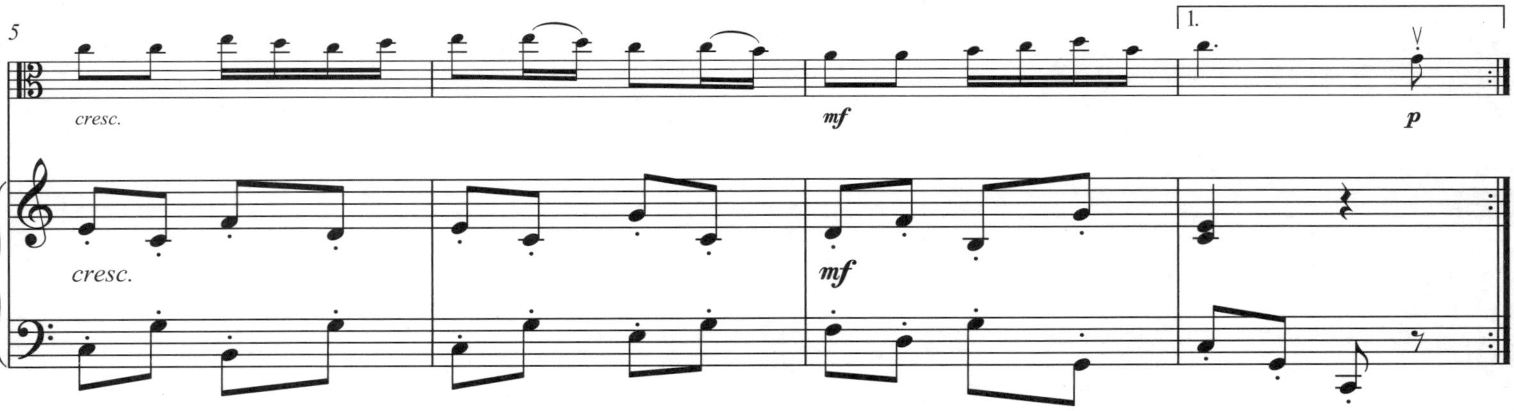

* harmonic

GAGLIARDO

This piece is a galliard: a dance pattern of hops and jumps. Try to reflect this
lightness when you play it and imagine the jumps in bars 4, 12, 16 and so on.

Pam Wedgwood

D.C. al Fine

LA SERENATA

Braga was an Italian cellist and composer. This piece, sometimes known as
'The Angel's Serenade', was originally written for voice and cello accompaniment.

Gaetano Braga
(1829–1907)

TRINITY REPERTOIRE LIBRARY

VIOLA

All Sorts

GRADES 2–3

Selected and edited by Mary Cohen

VIOLA PART

TRINITY COLLEGE LONDON
89 Albert Embankment London SE1 7TP

PRINCE OF DENMARK'S MARCH

Imagine a grand occasion at court when you play this, with everyone
dressed in fine clothes and music provided by trumpets and drums.

Jeremiah Clarke
(c.1670–1707)

THEME FROM POLOVTSIAN DANCES

The Russian composer Borodin wrote this piece as part of a ballet scene
within his opera *Prince Igor*.

Alexander Borodin
(1833–1887)

ROBIN'S RETREAT

This piece is based on a popular sixteenth-century dance style called an allemande.
Two lines of people dance towards each other, circle around and cross to the other side.

Pam Wedgwood

FISHER LADDIE

A lot of decoration is woven around this tune, just like the
fisher laddie weaving his needle in and out as he mends the fishing nets.

Traditional (English)
unaccompanied

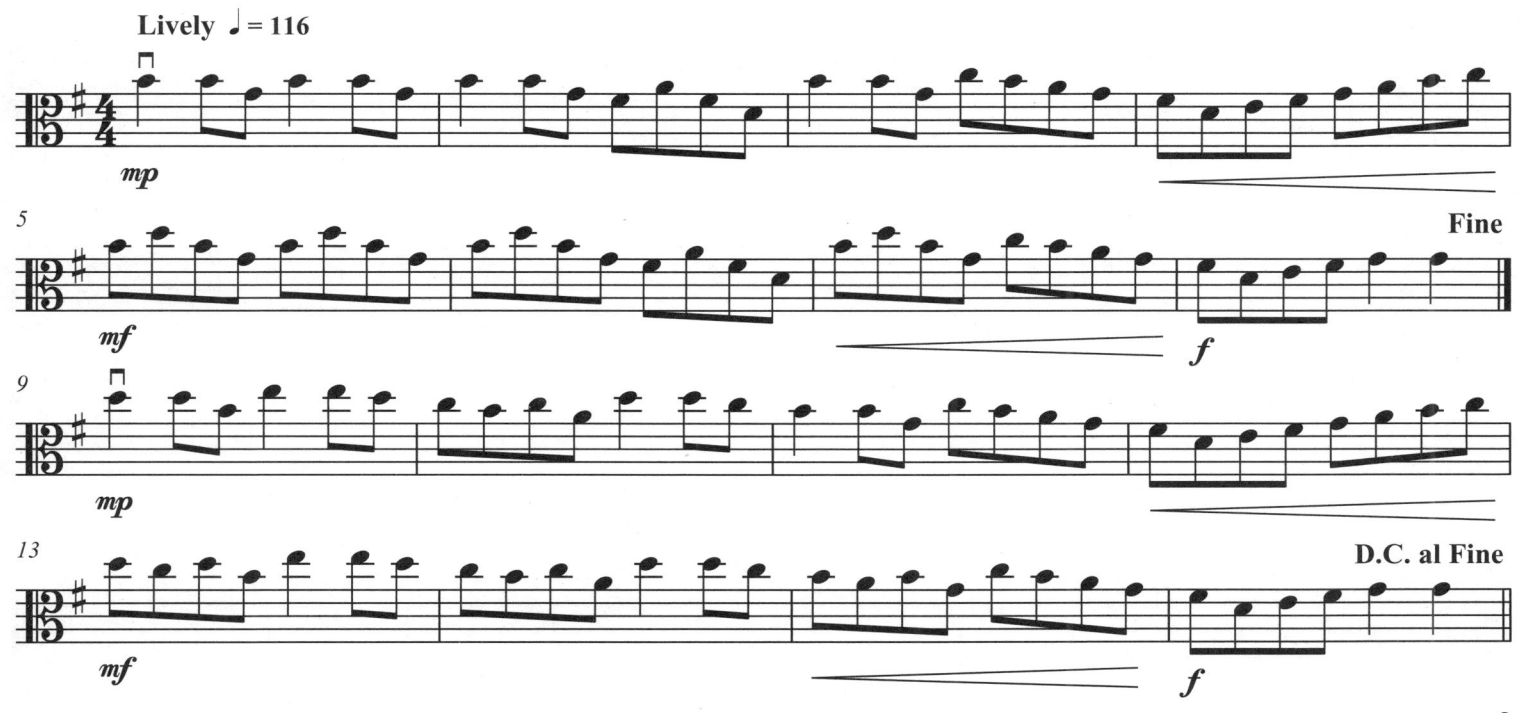

OUT 'N' ABOUT RAG

Mary Cohen

Music in 'ragged' time means that some beats are longer or shorter than you might expect. The most famous ragtime composer was Scott Joplin, who said 'you should never play them quick'.

LISON DORMAIT

This title means 'Lison was sleeping'. Imagine someone
tiptoeing past in bars 9 to 16, trying not to wake Lison.

Wolfgang Amadeus Mozart
(1756–1791)

MINUET

This was originally written for the baryton – a popular instrument in
Haydn's day. It had one set of strings to be plucked or bowed and
another set under the fingerboard which vibrated in sympathy.

Franz Joseph Haydn
(1732–1809)

DANCE OF THE BLESSED SPIRITS

This is one of Gluck's best-known pieces. It comes from his opera
Orpheus and Euridice.

Christoph von Gluck
(1714–1787)

SARABANDE

Corelli was an Italian violinist and composer. Although he wrote only a few works,
his style of violin playing set new standards and influenced many composers.

Arcangelo Corelli
(1653–1713)

PADDY O'RAFFERTY

This jig would be played at a ceilidh (pronounced 'kaylee'):
an Irish or Scottish party with traditional dancing and singing.

Traditional (Irish)
unaccompanied

MARCH FROM L'ARLÉSIENNE

This tune is based on a traditional carol from Provence called *The Three Kings*.
Imagine it's being played in a procession by a pipe and drum – fading into the
distance at the end.

Georges Bizet
(1838–1875)

PAVANE

Fauré wrote this piece for a big party in Paris. The guests dressed up in
historical costumes and danced to music played by a hidden band of musicians.

Gabriel Fauré
(1845–1924)

GAVOTTE *FROM* SUITE IN D

The Bach family produced several generations of musicians, of whom
Johann Sebastian was the most famous. As well as being a great
composer, J S Bach was a virtuoso organist.

Johann Sebastian Bach
(1685–1750)

9

THE DEATH OF ÅSE *FROM* PEER GYNT SUITE

Grieg was a Norwegian composer and pianist who had a great interest in his native folk music. Perhaps because of this, his music often contains unusual harmonies.

Edvard Grieg
(1843–1907)

BIG-BROTHER BLUES

Play this jazzy tune with lots of energy and rhythmic vitality.

Pam Wedgwood
unaccompanied

10

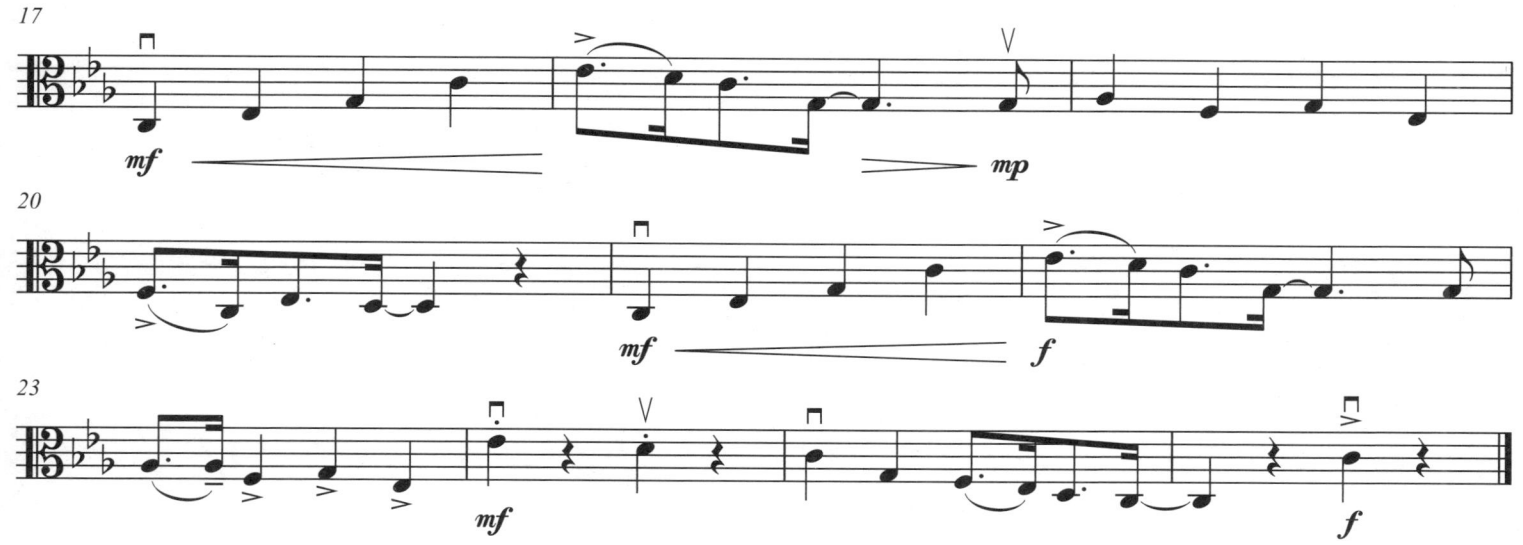

THE BIRDS GATHER AT DUSK

When the farmers hear the birds begin to gather at dusk,
it's the signal for the end of the long working day.

Mary Cohen
after a Chinese folk song

*harmonic

RONDO THEME *from op. 48*

Whilst a pupil of Haydn's, Pleyel wrote a piece that so impressed Haydn's patron, that the elder musician was presented with a carriage 'for having such a good pupil'. How fair was that?

Ignaz Pleyel
(1757–1831)

GAGLIARDO

This piece is a galliard: a dance pattern of hops and jumps. Try to reflect this lightness when you play it and imagine the jumps in bars 4, 12, 16 and so on.

Pam Wedgwood

17
4
f
24
p
29
1
4
2
f
4
37
p
mf
D.C. al Fine
2

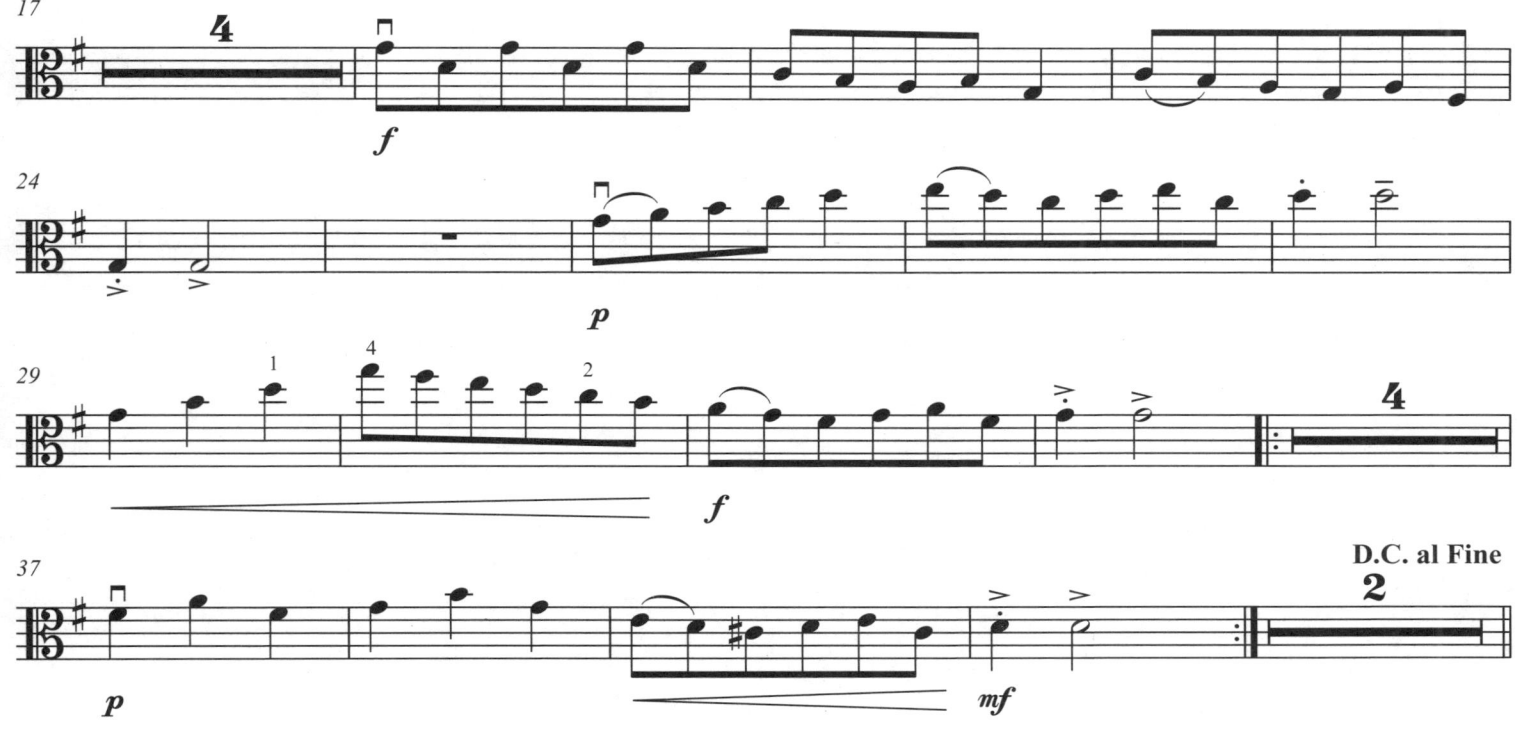

STICK DANCE

This little tune is traditionally played straight and then expanded by improvisation. A dancer waves a coloured stick decoratively in the air, drawing shapes which follow the musical ideas.

Traditional (Indian)
unaccompanied

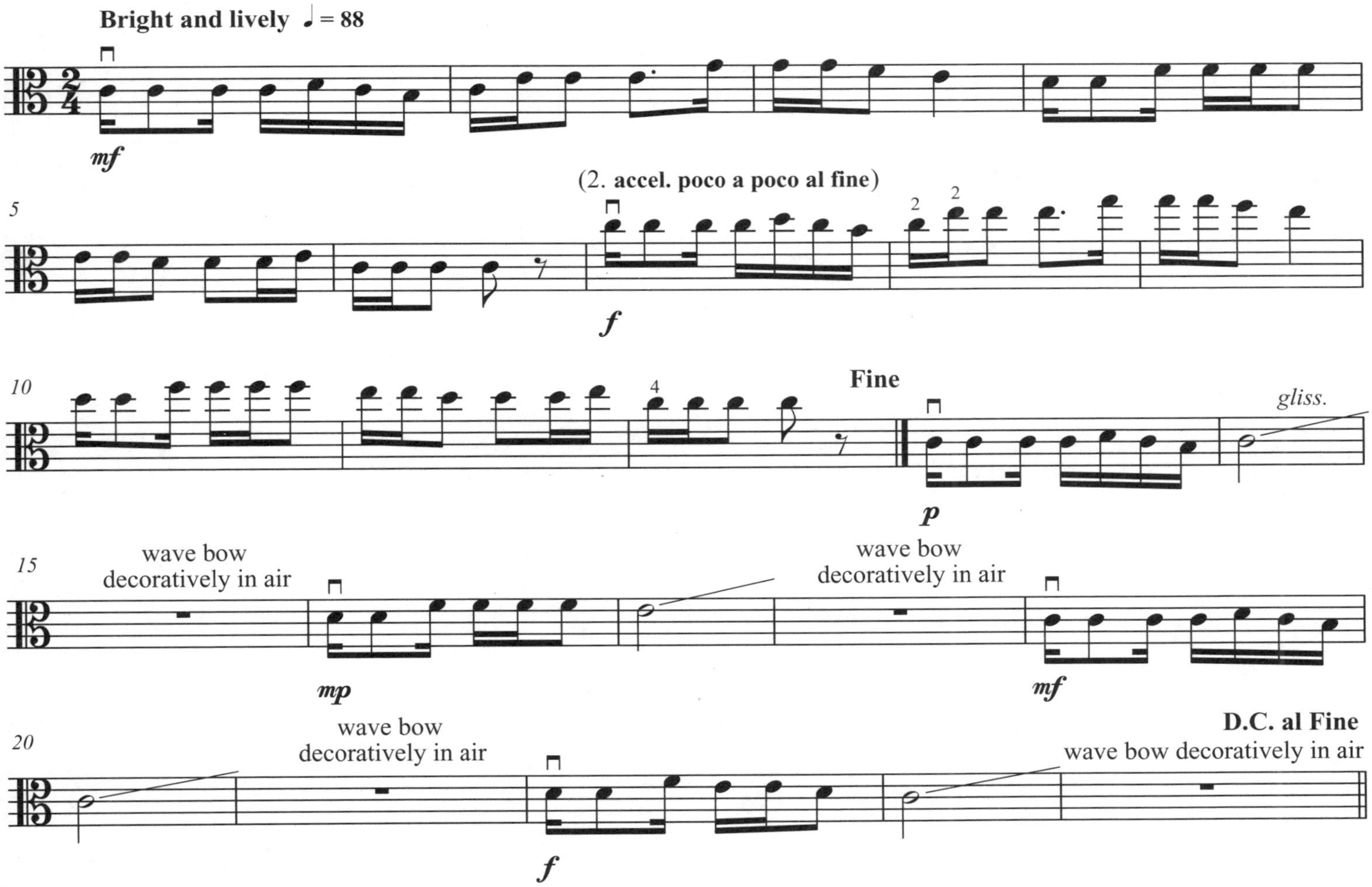
Bright and lively ♩ = 88
mf
(2. accel. poco a poco al fine)
5
f
10
Fine
p
gliss.
15
wave bow decoratively in air
mp
wave bow decoratively in air
mf
20
wave bow decoratively in air
f
D.C. al Fine
wave bow decoratively in air

LA SERENATA

Braga was an Italian cellist and composer. This piece, sometimes known as
'The Angel's Serenade', was originally written for voice and cello accompaniment.

Gaetano Braga
(1829–1907)

Contents

Published by:
Trinity College London
89 Albert Embankment
London SE1 7TP UK
T +44 (0)20 7820 6100
F +44 (0)20 7820 6161
E music@trinityguildhall.co.uk
www.trinityguildhall.co.uk

Printed in England by Halstan & Co. Ltd, Amersham, Bucks.
All Trinity Guildhall publications are available from your local music shop,
and may also be ordered directly from our exclusive distributor:

Faber Music Distribution Ltd, Burnt Mill, Elizabeth Way, Harlow CM20 2HX
T +44 (0)1279 82 89 82
F +44 (0)1279 82 89 83
sales@fabermusic.com
www.fabermusic.com